All Woman
volume four

AGAIN	2
ANYTHING FOR YOU	7
BABY LOVE	12
DIAMONDS ARE FOREVER	17
EVERGREEN	20
FOR YOUR EYES ONLY	29
HELP ME MAKE IT THROUGH THE NIGHT	32
HOPELESSLY DEVOTED TO YOU	34
I WANNA BE LOVED BY YOU	26
I WILL SURVIVE	38
I'LL BE THERE	48
IF I COULD TURN BACK TIME	50
MAD ABOUT THE BOY	56
THE MAN I LOVE	62
MY ONE TEMPTATION	43
PUPPET ON A STRING	66
A RAINY NIGHT IN GEORGIA	69
SEND IN THE CLOWNS	72
SMOOTH OPERATOR	75
SOPHISTICATED LADY	80
STAY WITH ME TILL DAWN	83
SWEET LOVE	86
THINK TWICE	89
TOUCH ME IN THE MORNING	92

Production:Sadie Cook
Published 1995

© International Music Publications Limited
Griffin House 161 Hammersmith Road London W6 8BS England

AGAIN

Words and Music by JANET JACKSON,
JAMES HARRIS III and TERRY LEWIS

ANYTHING FOR YOU

Words and Music by GLORIA ESTEFAN

BABY LOVE

Words and Music by BRIAN HOLLAND,
LAMONT DOZIER and EDDIE HOLLAND

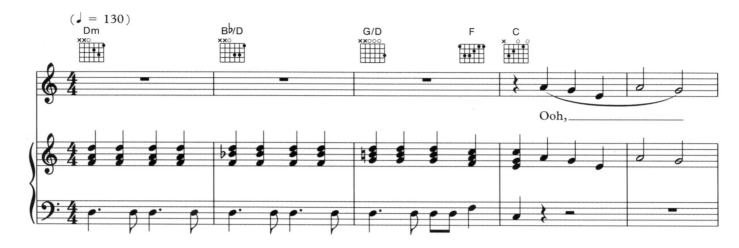

Ooh,

ba - by love, my ba - by love, I need__ you, oh how I need you,
Ba - by love, my ba - by love, why must we sep-ar - ate my love?

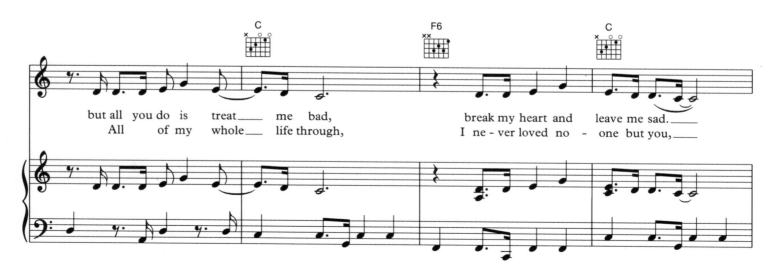

but all you do is treat__ me bad, break my heart and leave me sad.__
All of my whole__ life through, I ne - ver loved no - one but you,__

DIAMONDS ARE FOREVER

Words by DON BLACK
Music by JOHN BARRY

18

Diamonds Are Forever - 3 - 3

EVERGREEN

Words by PAUL WILLIAMS
Music by BARBRA STREISAND

22

I WANNA BE LOVED BY YOU

Words by BERT KALMAR
Music by HERBERT STOTHART and HARRY RUBY

REFRAIN   (See page 28 for Introduction and Verse)

INTRODUCTION AND VERSE

FOR YOUR EYES ONLY

Words by MICHAEL LEESON
Music by BILL CONTI

On - ly for you, _____ on - ly for you. _____

D.S. al Coda

Verse

2. For

Coda

On - ly for you, _____ for your eyes on - ly. _____

rit. e dim

HELP ME MAKE IT THROUGH THE NIGHT

Words and Music by
KRIS KRISTOFFERSON

Take the rib-bon from your hair, Shake it
Come and lay down by my side till the
Yes-ter-day is dead and gone and to-

loose and let it fall,_____ Lay-in' soft up-on my
ear-ly morn-in' light._____ All I'm ask-in' is your
mor-row's out of sight_____ And it's sad to be a-

1.
skin._____
time._____
lone._____

Like the shad-ows on the wall.

34

HOPELESSLY DEVOTED TO YOU

Words and Music by
JOHN FARRAR

35

I WILL SURVIVE

Words and Music by DINO FEKARIS
and FREDDIE PERREN

40

CHORUS

(2) It took all the strength I had ___ not to fall a-part, ___ kept try-in'

hard to mend the piec - es of my brok - en heart, and I spent oh so man-y nights just feel - in'

D.%. al Coda

sor ry for my -self. I used to cry ___ but now I hold my head up high and you see

CODA

I'll sur-vive. ___

MY ONE TEMPTATION

Words and Music by MICK LEESON,
PETER VALE and MILES WATERS

Life is tough ____ if you find ____
____ you can touch,

44

temp - ta - tion.

Noth-ing ev - er hap -pens till you

show your face a - round, can't tell you see that you turn my world a - round,— my

I'LL BE THERE

Words and Music by BERRY GORDY, HAL DAVIES,
WILLIE HUTCH and BOB WEST

2. I'll reach out my hand to you:
   I'll have faith in all you do.
   Just call my name and I'll be there.

3. Let me fill your heart with joy and laughter.
   Togetherness, girl, is all I'm after:
   Whenever you need me, I'll be there.
   I'll be there to protect you,
   With unselfish love that respects you.
   Just call my name, I'll be there.

IF I COULD TURN BACK TIME

Words and Music by
DIANE WARREN

52

MAD ABOUT THE BOY

Words and Music by
NOEL COWARD

60

THE MAN I LOVE

Music and Lyrics by
GEORGE GERSHWIN
and IRA GERSHWIN

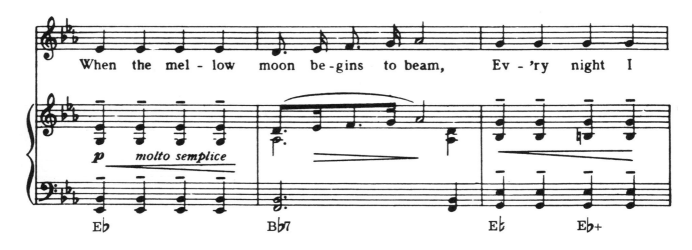

REFRAIN. (*slow*)

PUPPET ON A STRING

Words by PHIL COULTER
Music by BILL MARTIN

VERSE

A RAINY NIGHT IN GEORGIA

By TONY JOE WHITE

It still comes out the same; No mat-ter how you look at it, think of it; You just got to do your own thing.

D.C. al Fine

3. I find me a place in a box car,
   So I take out my guitar to pass some time;
   Late at night when it's hard to rest,
   I hold your picture to my chest, and I'm all right;
   (CHORUS)

SEND IN THE CLOWNS

Words and Music by
STEPHEN SONDHEIM

74

SMOOTH OPERATOR

Words and Music by
ADU and ST JOHN

76

SOPHISTICATED LADY

Words and Music by DUKE ELLINGTON,
IRVING MILLS and MITCHELL PARISH

STAY WITH ME TILL DAWN

Words and Music by JUDIE TZUKE
and MIKE PAXMAN

keep - ing me from some - one_____ I want to____ know_____ } But I
feel - ing that I've just got_____ to break out and say_____

need____ you to-night,_____ need you to- night.__ Yes I need____ you to- night,_____

need you to - night.__ And I'll show__ you a sun - set,__ if you'll stay with me till dawn.

SWEET LOVE

Words and Music by ANITA BAKER,
LOUIS A JOHNSON and GARY BIAS

88

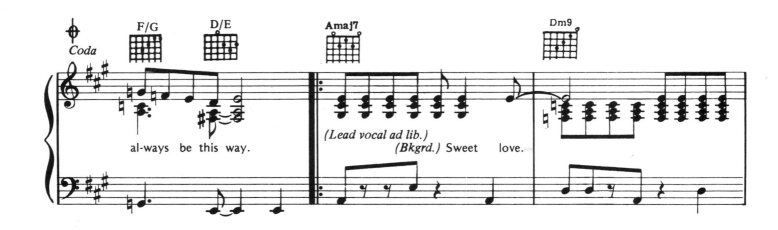

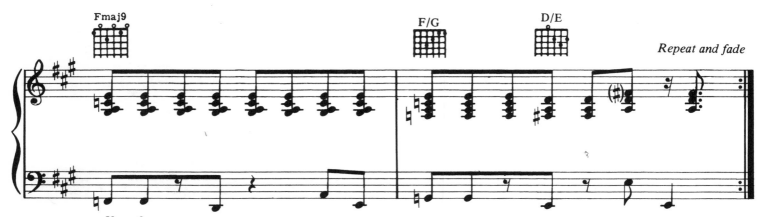

Verse 2:
Your heart has called me closer to you.
I will be all that you need.
Just trust in what we're feeling.
Never leave, 'cause baby, I believe
In this love. *(To Chorus:)*

Verse 3:
How sweet this dream, how lovely, baby.
Stay right here, never fear.
I will be all that you need.
Never leave, 'cause baby, I believe
In this love. *(To Chorus:)*

Coda = twice round, ending on A7 chord.

THINK TWICE

Words and Music by
PETE SINFIELD
and ANDY HILL

Verse 2:
Baby, think twice for the sake of our love, for the memory,
For the fire and the faith that was you and me.
Baby, I know it ain't easy when your soul cries out for higher ground,
'Cos when you're halfway up, you're always halfway down.
But baby, this is serious.
Are you thinking 'bout you or us?
(To Chorus:)

Chorus 4:
Don't do what you're about to do.
My everything depends on you,
And whatever it takes, I'll sacrifice.
Before you roll those dice,
Baby, think twice.

TOUCH ME IN THE MORNING

Words and Music by RONALD MILLER
and MICHAEL MASSER

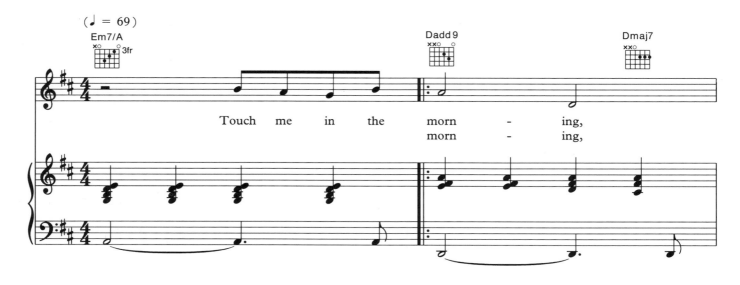

Touch me in the morn - ing,
morn - ing,

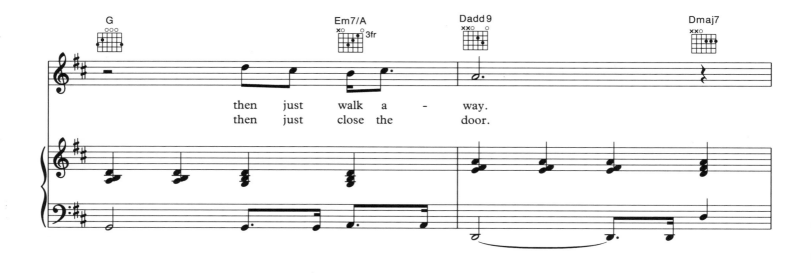

then just walk a - way.
then just close the door.

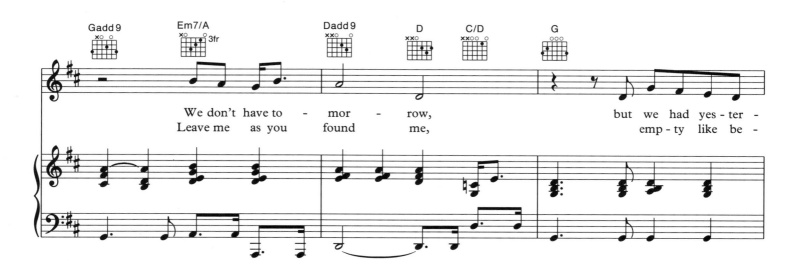

We don't have to - mor - row,
Leave me as you found me,

but we had yes - ter -
emp - ty like be -

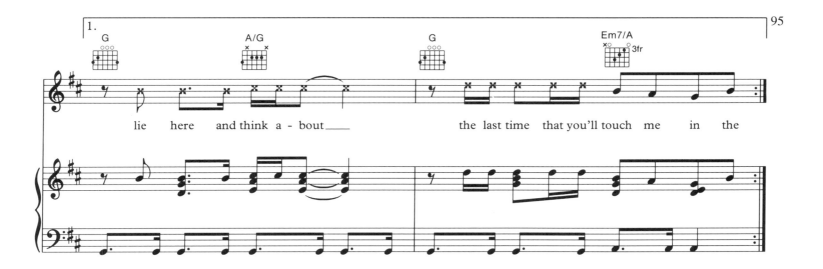

lie here and think a - bout___ the last time that you'll touch me in the

hold you un - til the time your hands reach out and touch me in the

morn - ing, then just walk a -

Morn-ings were blue_ and gold_ and we could feel one an - o - ther_ liv - ing.___

Reproduced and printed by
Halstan & Co. Ltd., Amersham, Bucks., England